EASY START

The secret and The birthday surprise

Series editor: Keith Gaines

Illustrated by Margaret de Souza

The secret   page 2

The birthday surprise   page 12

Nelson

The secret

Kim was playing at May-Ling's house.

"It will soon be my birthday,"
said May-Ling.
"I hope someone will give me a new bat.
My old bat is broken."

"I'll give May-Ling a new bat,"
said Kim.
"I'll save up my money and
I'll buy a new bat for May-Ling.

It will be a secret.
It will be a surprise
on May-Ling's birthday."

Kim's Dad gave her some money.

"Here you are, Kim," he said.
"You can buy some sweets with that."

"No," said Kim.
"I won't buy sweets.
I'm going to save my money.
I can't tell you
why I'm going to save it.
It's a secret."

Kim's Mum gave her some money too.

"Here you are, Kim," she said.
"You can buy a toy with that."

"No," said Kim.
"I won't buy a toy.
I'm going to save my money.
I can't tell you
why I'm going to save it.
It's a secret."

"It's May-Ling's birthday soon,"
said Kim.
"She is having a party.
I'm going to buy her a present.

Will you come to the toy shop with me,
Grandad?
I want to buy a present for May-Ling."

They went to the shop and got a big brown bat.

"This will be a surprise for May-Ling," said Kim.

The birthday surprise

"Happy birthday, May-Ling,"
said Kim.

"Come in, Kim,"
said May-Ling's Mum.

"I've got a present for May-Ling,"
said Kim.

"Thank you, Kim,"
said May-Ling's Mum.
"I'll put it here.
May-Ling will open the presents after tea."

All the children sat down for
the party tea.
They had sandwiches
and sausages
and red jelly
and pink cakes
and milk.

After tea,
they played some games.
Rob won a prize and
Jan won a prize.

"It's time to open the presents now," said May-Ling's Mum.
"Come on, May-Ling.

This one is from Jan,"
said May-Ling's Mum.

"It's a lovely doll,"
said May-Ling.
"Thank you, Jan."

"This one is from Rob,"
said May-Ling's Mum.

"It's a little toy dog,"
said May-Ling.
"Thank you, Rob."

"This is from me and Dad,"
said May-Ling's Mum.

"It's a new bat," said May-Ling.
"It's just what I wanted.
Thank you, Mum.
Thank you, Dad."

"This one is from Kim,"
said May-Ling's Mum.

"It's a new bat," said Kim.
"I've got you a bat, too."

"Don't be upset, Kim,"
said May-Ling's Mum.

"Now you have got two new bats, May-Ling.
You can both play."